CRAB COOKERY

By
Sherri Eldridge

Illustrations by
Fred Hartman

Crab Cookery

Published by:
Harvest Hill Press
P.O. Box 55
Salisbury Cove, Maine 04672
207-288-8900

ISBN: 1-886862-41-9

First printing: June 2002

PRINTED IN CANADA
ON ACID-FREE PAPER

The recipes in this book were created with the goal of reducing fat, calories, cholesterol and sodium. They also present a variety of fresh healthy foods, to be prepared with love and eaten with pleasure.

CREDITS:

Front Cover Crabs Watercolor: Kim Henson

Cover Design and Layout: Sherri Eldridge

Text Typesetting and Proofreading:
Bill Eldridge and Toni Litvinchyk

Text Line Art: Fred Hartman

PREFACE

Until recently, shellfish was forbidden to people on low cholesterol diets. After extensive research, we now know that the type of cholesterol and fats found in fish and shellfish do not raise but actually lower cholesterol levels! That makes shellfish a heart-healthy choice.

Shellfish are divided into two classes: crustaceans and mollusks. Crustaceans are sea animals with hard-crusted bodies which are segmented and joined together by flexible membranes. Because the bodies are hard and the animals grow as long as they live, periodically the old body must be shed. With crabs, this results in one of the great delicacies - soft-shelled crabs.

Crabs are ubiquitous along north american shores. Blue Crabs are dominant along the east coast and Gulf, with the bulk of the population in Chesapeake Bay. Stone Crabs are Florida's jewel, as is the King Crab in Alaska. Dungeness Crab is from the west coast, and the Snow Crab from the northwest. Off the coasts of New England and the maritimes, Rock and Jonah Crabs are harvested.

CONTENTS

Crab Omelet

SERVES 2

2 eggs
2 egg whites
pinch of salt
1 teaspoon butter
3 tablespoons finely chopped celery
2 tablespoons finely chopped chives
1 teaspoon tomato purée
½ teaspoon sherry
¼ teaspoon Worcestershire sauce
¼ teaspoon sugar
¼ lb. crabmeat
fresh ground pepper to taste

Serving: 1/2 omelet
Protein: 21.5 gm
Carbs: 3 gm
Sodium: 362 mg
Calories: 166
Fat: 7 gm
Cholesterol: 272 mg
Calcium: 95 mg

Beat eggs, egg whites and salt in a bowl.

In a nonstick skillet over medium heat, melt butter and sauté celery and chives for 5 minutes. Stir in all other ingredients, expect beaten eggs and cook 1 minute.

Pour egg mixture into skillet, tip pan to spread evenly. Cook until eggs are firm, about 3 minutes. Serve hot.

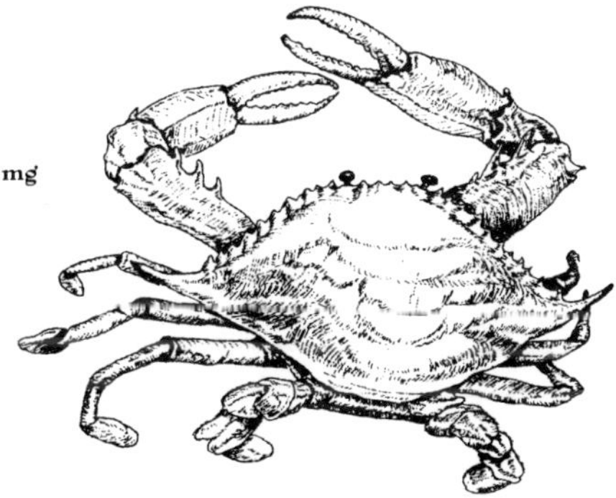

Easy Crab Paté

SERVES 6

1 small onion
1 tablespoon butter
3 tablespoons almond slivers
1 tablespoon brandy
½ lb. crabmeat
¼ teaspoon ground mace
pinch of salt
6 oz. soften nonfat cream cheese

Serving: 4 tablespoons	Calories: 113
Protein: 13 gm	Fat: 4.5 gm
Carbs: 4 gm	Cholesterol: 44 mg
Sodium: 294 mg	Calcium: 105 mg

Delicious served with french bread, melba toast or crackers.

Finely dice onion. Heat butter in skillet over moderate heat. Brown almonds in oil, remove with slotted spoon, and purée in food processor. Leave ground almonds in processor.

Sauté onion in the hot oil until translucent. Add brandy, crabmeat, mace and salt. Cook for 1 minute. Scrape mixture into food processor, add cream cheese and process until smooth.

Scrape paté into dish, cover with wax paper and chill until ready to use. Serve at room temperature.

Spicy Crab Dip

- 1½ cups plain nonfat yogurt
- 2 oz. softened nonfat cream cheese
- 1 tablespoon Dijon mustard
- 1 tablespoon low-salt catsup
- 2 teaspoons lemon juice
- ½ teaspoon dried thyme
- ½ teaspoon Worcestershire sauce
- ¼ teaspoon black pepper
- ¼ teaspoon hot sauce
- ¼ cup finely diced red pepper
- ¼ cup finely diced green pepper
- ¼ cup finely diced green onions
- ¾ lb. crabmeat

SERVES 6

Line a fine sieve with cheesecloth or paper towels. Fill with yogurt. Allow moisture to drain from yogurt for 20 minutes. Scrape into mixing bowl.

Add all remaining ingredients to bowl, except peppers, onions and crab. Beat until smooth.

Stir in peppers and onions. Gently fold in crabmeat. Refrigerate at least 1 hour. Allow to warm to room temperature before serving.

Great with vegetable crudites and crisp crackers.

Serving: 1/2 cup	Calories: 113
Protein: 16.5 gm	Fat: 1.5 gm
Carbs: 8 gm	Cholesterol: 59 mg
Sodium: 282 mg	Calcium: 210 mg

Crab Puffs

nonfat spray cooking oil
2 tablespoons finely chopped green onions
½ cup grated lowfat cheddar cheese
8 oz. softened nonfat cream cheese
½ cup nonfat mayonnaise
1 tablespoon lemon juice
¼ teaspoon garlic powder
¼ teaspoon cayenne pepper
pinch of salt
1 lb. crabmeat
20 phyllo dough sheets (about 1 lb.)

Serving: 1 puff	Calories: 51
Protein: 4 gm	Fat: 1 gm
Carbs: 6 gm	Cholesterol: 12 mg
Sodium: 145 mg	Calcium: 30 mg

MAKES 40 PUFFS

Preheat oven to 375°. Spray a baking sheet with nonstick oil.

Beat all ingredients in a mixing bowl, except crab and dough, until smooth. Fold in crabmeat.

Spread phyllo dough sheets on a dry surface and cut lengthwise into four strips. Lay one strip on a sheet of waxed paper, spray with oil, cover with second strip and spray with oil. Spread 1 tablespoon prepared filling in lower right corner of strip. Fold dough so bottom right corner becomes parallel with the left side, forming a triangle. Continue to fold up in triangles, like folding a flag, until entire strip is used. Place on baking sheet with folded side down. Fold up all puffs. Bake 15-20 minutes, until golden brown. Serve hot.

West Indies Salad

SERVES 4

1 small yellow onion
1 lb. crabmeat
¼ teaspoon black pepper
¼ cup canola oil
6 tablespoons cider vinegar
½ cup crushed ice and water
4 large lettuce leaves
1 teaspoon paprika

Serving: 1/4 recipe	Calories: 186
Protein: 23 gm	Fat: 8.5 gm
Carbs: 3 gm	Cholesterol: 113 mg
Sodium: 317 mg	Calcium: 124 mg

Peel and finely dice onion. Spread half of the diced onion in a flat bottomed mixing bowl.

Spread crabmeat over onion in the bowl. Sprinkle remaining onion over crabmeat, then pepper. Pour oil, vinegar and then ice water over crab. Cover and marinate at least 4 hours, but preferably overnight in refrigerator.

Place a lettuce leaf on each plate. Lightly toss marinated crab and pour off excess liquid. Place one-quarter crab mixture on each plate. Sprinkle each salad with paprika before serving.

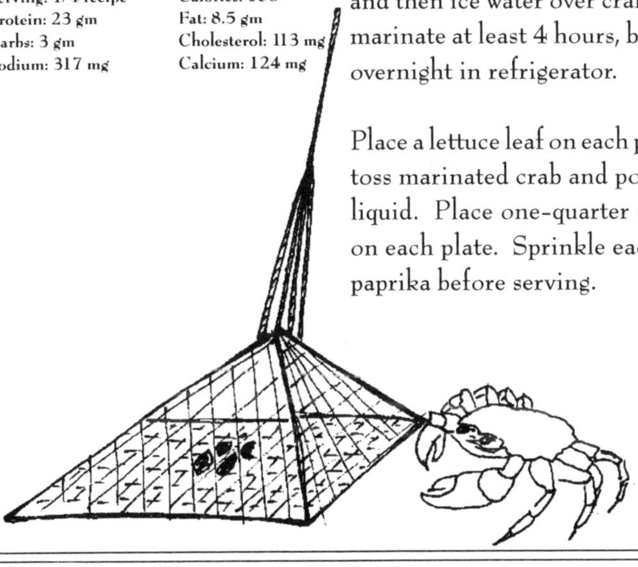

All About Crabs

The crab is one of the oldest species on earth, with the Horseshoe Crab dating back over 200 million years. Edible crabs all have 5 pairs of legs, the front two being large pinchers. Females are distinguished from males by the shape in the center of their under shell - females are heart shaped while males have a small triangle with a spire.

Blue Crabs, whose Latin name means beautiful swimmer, range in size from 3½ to 5½ inches. The Blue Crab has a blue-green colored shell that turns red when cooked. Dungeness Crabs must be at least 6¼ inches to be legally caught. They are a brownish purple hue, and usually weigh 2 to 4 pounds. The giant of the crabs is the King, with a leg span of 2 to 5 feet and weighing 10 to 15 pounds. Most of its meat is in the legs and claws, which can be frozen to extend storage time. The Snow Crab is smaller than the King, but much more numerous. Snow Crabs, or their meat, are commonly found in markets throughout the country. When caught, a Stone Crab has a claw removed, then the crab itself is returned to the sea, where it will grow a replacement leg.

Crab & Broccoli Soup

SERVES 6

- 1 tablespoon canola oil
- 1 cup diced onion
- 5 tablespoons flour
- 4 cups fish broth
- 2 cups diced red potatoes
- ½ cup white wine
- ½ tablespoon Worcestershire sauce
- ½ teaspoon sage
- ¼ teaspoon nutmeg
- ¼ teaspoon pepper
- dash hot sauce
- 2½ cups lowfat milk
- ½ cup grated lowfat cheddar cheese
- 1½ cups broccoli florets
- ¾ lb. crabmeat
- 2 tablespoons lemon juice
- 1 tablespoon sherry

Heat oil in stock pot, then sauté onions 5 minutes. Add flour, stir and cook for 2 minutes. Add broth, potatoes, wine, Worcestershire sauce and spices. Simmer 30 minutes. Spoon potatoes and onions into blender with 1 cup of cooked liquid. Blend until smooth, then return to pot. Add milk and cheese, simmer about 10 minutes.

In a separate pot, steam broccoli for 5 minutes. Add broccoli, crab, lemon juice and sherry to soup. Heat thoroughly but do not boil. Serve hot.

Serving: 1 1/2 cups	Calories: 275
Protein: 24 gm	Fat: 7 gm
Carbs: 26 gm	Cholesterol: 65 mg
Sodium: 555 mg	Calcium: 262 mg

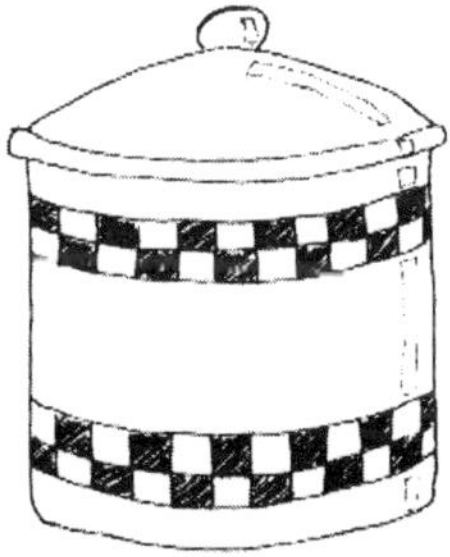

She-Crab Soup

12 blue she-crabs
1½ tablespoons butter
2 tablespoons diced onion
3 tablespoons unbleached flour
4 cups scalded lowfat milk
1 teaspoon grated lemon peel
½ teaspoon mace
½ teaspoon white pepper
pinch of salt
2 tablespoons dry sherry
1 tablespoon parsley

Serving: 1/4 recipe
Protein: 20.5 gm
Carbs: 18 gm
Sodium: 384 mg
Calories: 235
Fat: 8 gm
Cholesterol: 71 mg
Calcium: 362 mg

SERVES 4

Steam crabs, pick meat and reserve roe. Heat butter in a stock pot on medium heat, then sauté onions until translucent. Add flour and stir while cooking for 2 minutes. Remove pot from heat, and whisk in milk until smooth. Add lemon peel, mace, pepper, salt and crabmeat. Return to burner on low heat, cook for 20 minutes. Stir in sherry when ready to serve.

Divide roe among 4 bowls, ladle in soup and sprinkle parsley over each bowl.

Gumbo

SERVES 4

- 4 dried hot red chilies
- 1 lemon
- 3 bay leaves
- 1½ teaspoons thyme
- 2 pinches salt
- 7 quarts water
- 12 live blue crabs
- 1 tablespoon canola oil
- 3 tablespoons unbleached flour
- ½ cup chopped onions
- 1½ teaspoons mashed garlic
- ½ lb. sliced okra
- ¾ cup chopped green pepper
- 1 teaspoon cayenne
- ½ teaspoon Tabasco
- ¾ lb. cooked, peeled and deveined shrimp
- 6 cups cooked rice

Serving: 1/4 recipe	Calories: 557
Protein: 38.5 gm	Fat: 6.5 gm
Carbs: 85 gm	Cholesterol: 178 mg
Sodium: 440 mg	Calcium: 260 mg

Remove seeds from chilies. Slice lemon into ¼ inch rounds. Put lemon, chilies, bay leaves, thyme and salt into pot. Heat water in large stock pot to boil. Cook crabs for 7 minutes, remove to cool. Boil water down to 3 quarts, then strain, reserving liquid. Pick meat and roe from crabs, setting both aside.

Brown oil and flour in large pot over low heat for 5 minutes. Add onions and garlic to roux, cook 5 minutes. Add okra, green pepper and strained liquid to pot, and stirring constantly, bring to a boil. Add cayenne, Tabasco and crabmeat, cook over low heat 1 hour. Stir in shrimp, cook 3 minutes more.

Mound hot rice in soup bowls and ladle gumbo around rice in each bowl.

Quick Gumbo

2 tablespoons butter
1 lb. sliced okra
½ cup chopped onion
½ cup chopped pepper
½ teaspoon mashed garlic
4 tablespoons flour
4 cups fish broth
2 cups dry white wine
2 cups chopped tomatoes
½ teaspoon thyme
1 teaspoon black pepper
6 springs parsley
1 bay leaf
1 lb. peeled deveined shrimp
1 lb. crabmeat
12 shucked fresh oysters
2 teaspoons lemon juice
2 teaspoons Worcestershire sauce
¼ teaspoon Tabasco
3 cups cooked rice

Serving: 1/6 recipe
Calories: 440
Protein: 38.5 gm
Fat: 8.5 gm
Carbs: 39 gm
Cholesterol: 211 mg
Sodium: 548 mg
Calcium: 228 mg

SERVES 6

Heat butter in a large saucepan over moderate heat. Add okra and cook until white threads no longer appear. Add onion, pepper and garlic, cook 5 minutes. Add flour, stirring constantly, and cook 5 minutes more. Stir in broth and wine. Add tomatoes, thyme, pepper, parsley and bay leaf. Bring to a boil, reduce heat to low and simmer ½ hour. Add shrimp, crab and oysters, cook 8 minutes more. Stir in lemon juice, Worcestershire sauce and Tabasco. Serve in bowls with ½ cup rice.

How to Crack Crabs

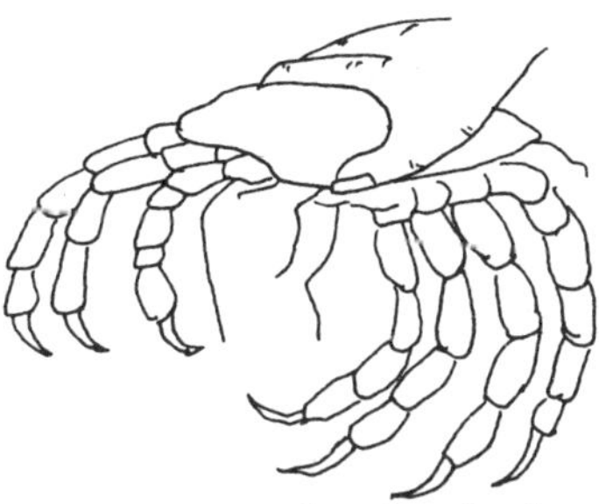

Remove the back by gripping the body in one hand, and using the other hand to pry off the shell.

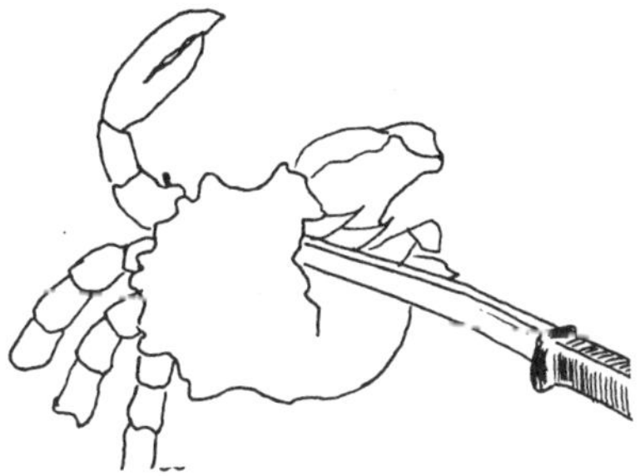

Use a short sturdy knife to remove the gills from the crab's underside. Wash out intestines and spongy matter.

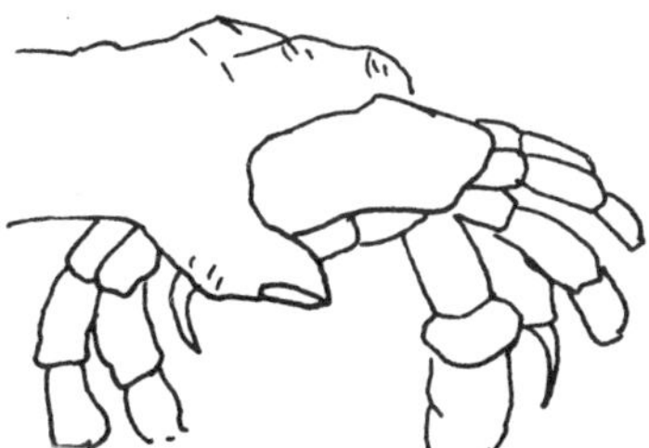

Break off claws and legs from the body. Use nut crackers or a mallet to crack open claws and legs. A pick or small knife can be used to pick out the meat.

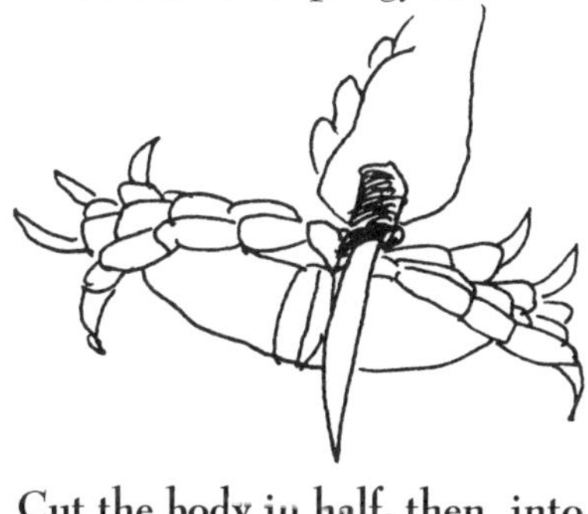

Cut the body in half, then into smaller parts. Use a pick or small pointy knife to remove lump meat from the back sections, and pry remaining meat from body.

Steamed Crabs

SERVES 4

1 cup cider vinegar
3 cups water
12-16 live crabs
1 cup seafood seasoning

Seafood Seasoning:
3 cups kosher salt
6 tablespoons black pepper
1 tablespoon cayenne
3 tablespoons dry mustard
1 tablespoon mustard seeds
1 tablespoon ground ginger
2 teaspoons paprika
Mix and store in sealed jar.

Serving: 3-4 crabs	Calories: 73
Protein: 15 gm	Fat: 1 gm
Carbs: 0 gm	Cholesterol: 66 mg
Sodium: 246 mg	Calcium: 75 mg

Set a rack in the bottom of a 12 quart enamel or stainless steel pot. Add vinegar and water to pot.

Make one layer of crabs on rack and sprinkle with 4 tablespoons seafood seasoning. Continue layering crabs and sprinkling with seasoning.

Bring liquid to a boil, then cover pot. Cook 20-25 minutes, until crabs are red. Serve immediately.

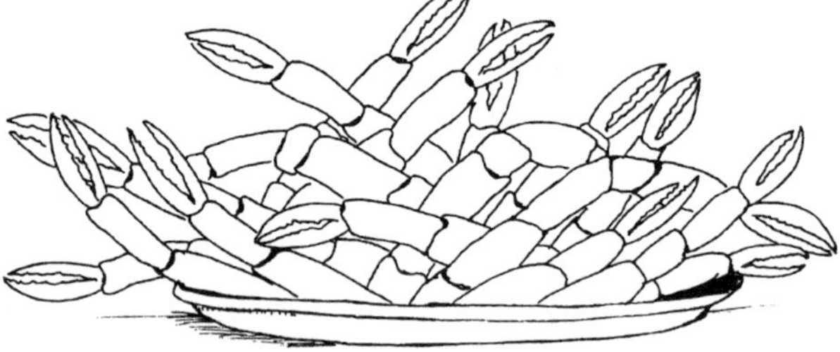

Perfect Soft Shell Crabs

SERVES 4

- **8 medium or 12 small fresh soft-shell crabs**
- **1 cup unbleached flour**
- **1 tablespoon unsalted butter**
- **3 tablespoons canola oil**
- **2 tablespoons lemon juice**
- **4 lemon wedges**

Serving: 1/4 recipe	Calories: 160
Protein: 10 gm	Fat: 7 gm
Carbs: 15 gm	Cholesterol: 41 mg
Sodium: 124 mg	Calcium: 43 mg

Wash crabs in cold water. Using scissors, snip off heads about ½ inch behind eyes. Turn crabs over, remove triangular apron and scrap out spongy gills. Wash and pat dry. Dredge each crab in flour.

In a large skillet, melt butter and oil over high heat. Sauté crabs until crisp, about 7 minutes, turning several times with tongs. Store crabs on plate in warm oven. When all the crabs are cooked, add lemon juice to skillet, swirl and pour over crabs. Serve hot with lemon wedges.

Snip off head about ½ inch behind eyes.

Turn the crab over to remove triangular apron.

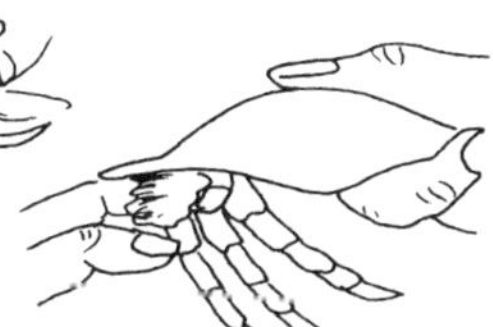

Lift the pointed ends of the shell to scrape out spongy gills.

Crab & Pasta Sauté

2 garlic cloves
1 serrano chili
1 tablespoon olive oil
2 cups white wine or fish broth
1 tablespoon butter
1 lb. crabmeat
1 lb. cavatelli pasta
2 quarts water
pinch of salt
pepper to taste

Serving: 1/4 recipe
Protein: 29.5 gm
Carbs: 33 gm
Sodium: 338 mg
Calories: 406
Fat: 8.5 gm
Cholesterol: 157 mg
Calcium: 147 mg

SERVES 4

Peel garlic and slice into thin slivers. Seed, then thinly slice serrano chili.

Heat oil in a large skillet over medium heat. Sauté garlic and chili 3 minutes. Add wine and butter, then bring to a boil. Add crabmeat, remove from heat.

Boil pasta in water until al dente, drain and add to crab mixture. Return skillet to medium heat, add salt and pepper, and cook until liquid is absorbed. Serve hot.

Crabcakes

6 slices white bread
1 tablespoon canola oil
1 tablespoon butter
¼ cup chopped green onions
¼ cup chopped red pepper
2 egg whites
2 tablespoons lowfat mayonnaise
1 tablespoon Dijon mustard
¼ teaspoon Tabasco
2 tablespoons chopped fresh parsley
¼ teaspoon cayenne
1 lb. crabmeat

Serving: 1/4 recipe	Calories: 245
Protein: 27.5 gm	Fat: 7.5 gm
Carbs: 15 gm	Cholesterol: 119 mg
Sodium: 586 mg	Calcium: 160 mg

SERVES 4

Trim crust off bread slices, then bake in 350° oven until golden brown on each side in . Crush with rolling pin to make bread crumbs.

Heat 1 teaspoon of oil and butter in large skillet and sauté onion and pepper for 5 minutes. In a bowl whisk cooked onion and pepper with egg whites, mayonnaise, mustard, Tabasco, parsley, cayenne and 3 tablespoons of bread crumbs. Fold in crabmeat, divide into 8 equal portions. Form patties in your hands, dredge in bread crumbs, and chill on waxed paper for 1 hour.

Heat remaining 2 teaspoons of oil and butter in a large nonstick skillet, and fry patties until golden. Serve hot with a selection of sauces.

Tartar Sauce

MAKES 1 CUP

2 tablespoons wine vinegar
1 teaspoon dry mustard
pinch of cayenne
¾ cup nonfat mayonnaise
2 tablespoons pickle relish
1 tablespoon chopped chives
1 tablespoon parsley
1 teaspoon chopped capers
1 shallot, finely diced

Whisk vinegar, mustard and cayenne into mayonnaise. Stir in remaining ingredients. Chill for at least 2 hours before serving.

Serving: 3 tablespoons	Calories: 24
Protein: 0 gm	Fat: 0 gm
Carbs: 5 gm	Cholesterol: 0 mg
Sodium: 224 mg	Calcium: 3 mg

Red Chipolte Sauce

MAKES 1¼ CUP

½ cup nonfat cottage cheese
½ cup nonfat yogurt
1 seeded diced chipolte chili
1 peeled seeded tomato
3 tablespoons diced cilantro
1 teaspoon lime juice

Process cottage cheese, yogurt and chile in blender until smooth. Pour mixture into mixing bowl and stir in remaining ingredients. Chill at least 2 hours.

Serving: 2 tablespoons	Calories: 29
Protein: 3.5 gm	Fat: 0 gm
Carbs: 3 gm	Cholesterol: 1 mg
Sodium: 20 mg	Calcium: 48 mg

Dijon Sauce

MAKES 1 CUP

1 teaspoon canola oil
1 teaspoon butter
1 tablespoon diced shallots
1 tablespoon flour
1 cup white wine
2 tablespoons Dijon mustard
¼ teaspoon white pepper

Serving: 2 tablespoons	Calories: 39
Protein: .5 gm	Fat: 1.5 gm
Carbs: 2 gm	Cholesterol: 1 mg
Sodium: 28 mg	Calcium: 9 mg

Heat oil and butter in sauce pan over medium heat. Sauté shallots for 3 minutes, whisk in flour and cook for 2 minutes. Whisk in wine, mustard and pepper, stirring until smooth. Serve as a warm sauce.

Rémoulade Sauce

MAKES 1 CUP

1 hard-boiled egg
1 tablespoon finely chopped sour gherkin
2 teaspoons chopped capers 1 tablespoon parsley
1 garlic clove, mashed
¾ cup nonfat mayonnaise
1 teaspoon dried tarragon
1 teaspoon Dijon mustard

Serving: 2 tablespoons	Calories: 27
Protein: 1 gm	Fat: 1 gm
Carbs: 3 gm	Cholesterol: 27 mg
Sodium: 233 mg	Calcium: 8 mg

Finely dice the hard-boiled egg. In a mixing bowl, stir all ingredients together, mixing well. Cover and chill for at least 2 hours before serving.

The Healthy (for You) Crab

All shellfish, including crab, are a good source of omega-3 fatty acids. Two recent studies have shown that healthy people can minimize their risk of heart attack by eating two or more servings of foods high in omega-3 fatty acids each week. The most prominent fatty acids are DHA and EPA. These polyunsaturated fats are incorporated into the human body and form hormone-like substances which are believed to play a significant role in boosting the immune response, reducing the risk of cancer, and heart disease.

While shellfish are high in cholesterol, early research studies were unable to distinguish the good non-cholesterol sterols that are found in shellfish. This had given rise to the warnings about eating too much shellfish, which we now know not to be true.

Two trace elements important to health are also in crab: chromium which works with insulin to metabolize sugar and raise levels of HDL (a good cholesterol), and selenium, an antioxidant which detoxifies carcinogenic substances such as arsenic and mercury.

Deviled Crab

1 tablespoon butter
¼ cup diced onions
¼ cup diced red pepper
¼ cup diced green pepper
2 tablespoons flour
¾ cup lowfat milk blended with ¼ cup nonfat dry powdered milk
pinch of nutmeg
pinch of dry mustard
1 egg yolk, beaten
3 tablespoons dry sherry
½ teaspoon pepper
1 lb. crabmeat
½ cup bread crumbs

Serving: 1/4 recipe	Calories: 286
Protein: 29 gm	Fat: 7.5 gm
Carbs: 21 gm	Cholesterol: 177 mg
Sodium: 514 mg	Calcium: 271 mg

Served over hot boiled rice, this makes a wonderful meal!

SERVES 4

Preheat oven to 400°. Spray a 1-quart baking dish with nonstick oil.

Heat butter in a pan, add onions and peppers and sauté until onion is clear. Blend in flour. In a separate pot, bring milk to a boil and stir in onion and peppers. Remove from heat, stir in nutmeg and mustard. Whisk in egg yolk, sherry and pepper. Stir in crabmeat.

Transfer mixture to baking dish and sprinkle with bread crumbs. Bake until crab is hot and top is lightly browned.

Crab Mousse

SERVES 8

- 2 envelopes gelatin
- ¼ cup cold water
- 1 tablespoon butter
- 1 tablespoon canola oil
- 3 tablespoons flour
- ¾ cup lowfat milk
- ¾ cup fish broth
- 1 lb. crabmeat
- 1 tablespoon lemon juice
- 1 tablespoon chopped parsley
- 1 teaspoon dill
- ½ teaspoon paprika
- ½ teaspoon dry mustard
- ¼ teaspoon white pepper
- pinch of salt
- 1 cup nonfat evaporated milk, chilled in freezer

Dissolve gelatin in cold water. Heat butter and oil in sauce pan over medium heat, then stir in flour. In a separate pot, boil milk with broth. Whisk milk mixture into flour mixture until smooth. Whisk in gelatin until smooth. Remove from heat and stir in all other ingredients, except evaporated milk. Refrigerate until it begins to firm.

Whip evaporated milk until soft peaks form. Fold into chilled mixture. Pour crab mousse into mold, chill overnight.

Serving: 1/8 recipe	Calories: 144
Protein: 17 gm	Fat: 5 gm
Carbs: 8 gm	Cholesterol: 63 mg
Sodium: 276 mg	Calcium: 185 mg

Crab & Artichoke Soufflé

14 oz. can artichoke hearts
2 tablespoons cake flour
1 tablespoon canola oil
¼ cup finely diced onion
2 tablespoons cake flour
1½ cups lowfat milk
1 egg
7 egg whites
3 tablespoons fresh grated Parmesan cheese
pinch of white pepper
pinch of cayenne
¾ lb. crabmeat
½ teaspoon cream of tartar

Serving: 1/4 recipe	Calories: 294
Protein: 33 gm	Fat: 8 gm
Carbs: 23 gm	Cholesterol: 144 mg
Sodium: 536 mg	Calcium: 293 mg

SERVES 4

Preheat oven to 375°. Drain and chop artichoke hearts. Spray soufflé dish with nonstick oil, then dust with cake flour.

Heat oil in sauce pan and sauté onion for 5 minutes over medium heat. Sprinkle with flour, and stirring constantly, cook 2 minutes. Whisk milk into flour mixture until smooth and boiling. In a mixing bowl, whisk egg and 3 egg whites, then whisk in milk mixture and all other ingredients, except 4 egg whites and cream of tartar.

In a stainless steel mixing bowl, beat remaining 4 egg whites until soft peaks form. Beat in cream of tartar, then fold into crab mixture. Pour into soufflé dish and bake 45 minutes until puffed and golden on top. Serve piping hot.

Crab & Shrimp Callaloo

SERVES 8

1½ tablespoons olive oil
2 large onions
1 lb. fresh spinach
2 large tomatoes
6 cups fish broth
½ teaspoon pepper
½ teaspoon nutmeg
1 lb. crabmeat
1 lb. deveined peeled shrimp
¼ teaspoon Tabasco

Serving: 1/8 recipe	Calories: 203
Protein: 29.5 gm	Fat: 6.5 gm
Carbs: 7 gm	Cholesterol: 145 mg
Sodium: 578 mg	Calcium: 159 mg

Heat olive oil in pot. Peel and chop onions, then sauté for 5 minutes over medium heat. Clean and chop spinach. Peel and chop tomatoes. Add spinach, tomatoes, fish broth, pepper and nutmeg to onion sauté. Bring to a boil, reduce heat and simmer 20 minutes

Add crabmeat and shrimp, continue simmering for 8 minutes more. Add Tabasco, stir, and serve hot.

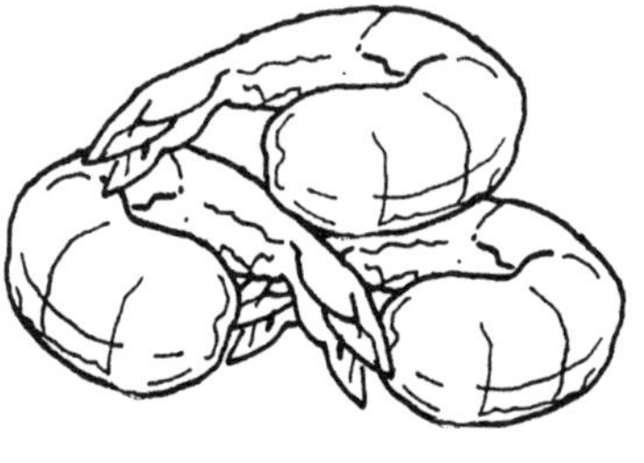

Crab Louis

SERVES 4

2 egg whites
½ cup nonfat mayonnaise
1 tablespoon chili sauce
1 teaspoon grated horseradish
1 tablespoon lemon juice
pinch of pepper
½ teaspoon Worcestershire sauce
1 tablespoon olive oil
1 tablespoon red wine vinegar
¼ cup finely chopped green pepper
2 tablespoons finely chopped green onions
1 cup shredded lettuce
1 lb. crabmeat

In a mixing bowl, beat egg whites until stiff. Beat in mayonnaise, chili sauce, horseradish, lemon juice, pepper and Worcestershire sauce.

In separate bowl, whisk olive oil and wine vinegar until blended, then whisk into mayonnaise sauce. Stir in chopped pepper and onions.

Spread lettuce on each plate. Mound crabmeat on lettuce. Divide Louis sauce over each serving.

Serving: 1/4 recipe	Calories: 185
Protein: 25 gm	Fat: 5.5 gm
Carbs: 7 gm	Cholesterol: 113 mg
Sodium: 644 mg	Calcium: 127 mg

Crab Quiche

SERVES 6

- 1 onion
- 1 red bell pepper
- ¾ lb. mushrooms
- 2 teaspoons canola oil
- 2 eggs
- 2 egg whites
- 1½ cups nonfat cottage cheese
- ¼ cup grated Parmesan
- ½ cup plain nonfat yogurt
- ¼ cup unbleached flour
- ¼ teaspoon cayenne
- ¼ teaspoon black pepper
- pinch of salt
- ¼ teaspoon Tabasco
- ¾ lb. crabmeat
- 6 oz. lowfat Swiss cheese, grated
- ¼ cup diced green onions

Preheat oven to 350°. Spray quiche pan or pie plate with nonstick oil. Peel and chop onion. Clean and seed pepper, finely dice. Slice mushrooms. Sauté onion and pepper for 5 minutes over medium heat in oil. Add mushrooms and sauté 5 minutes more.

Process eggs, cottage cheese, Parmesan, yogurt, flour, spices and Tabasco in blender until smooth. In a mixing bowl, combine vegetable sauté with blender mixture. Fold in crabmeat, Swiss cheese and green onions. Pour into quiche pan and bake 45 minutes, or until toothpick inserted in middle comes out clean.

Serving: 1/6 recipe	Calories: 263
Protein: 35 gm	Fat: 8.5 gm
Carbs: 13 gm	Cholesterol: 144 mg
Sodium: 394 mg	Calcium: 461 mg

Crab & Corn Custard

1 cup lowfat milk
1 cup nonfat evaporated milk
¼ cup nonfat powdered milk
2 eggs
2 egg whites
16 oz. can creamed corn, +unsalted
1 teaspoon Worcestershire sauce
1 teaspoon brown sugar
¼ teaspoon white pepper
½ lb. crabmeat

Serving: 1/4 recipe	Calories: 280
Protein: 26.5 gm	Fat: 5 gm
Carbs: 35 gm	Cholesterol: 168 mg
Sodium: 363 mg	Calcium: 391 mg

SERVES 4

Preheat oven to 325°. Spray a baking dish with nonstick cooking spray.

Heat milks in sauce pan over medium low heat. In a mixing bowl, whisk eggs. While whisking, pour warm milk in steady stream into eggs. Whisk in remaining ingredients, except crabmeat. Fold in crabmeat. Pour mixture into baking dish and set in middle of roasting pan. Pour hot water into roasting pan, to a depth half way up side of baking dish. Bake 1 hour, or until toothpick inserted in middle comes out clean.

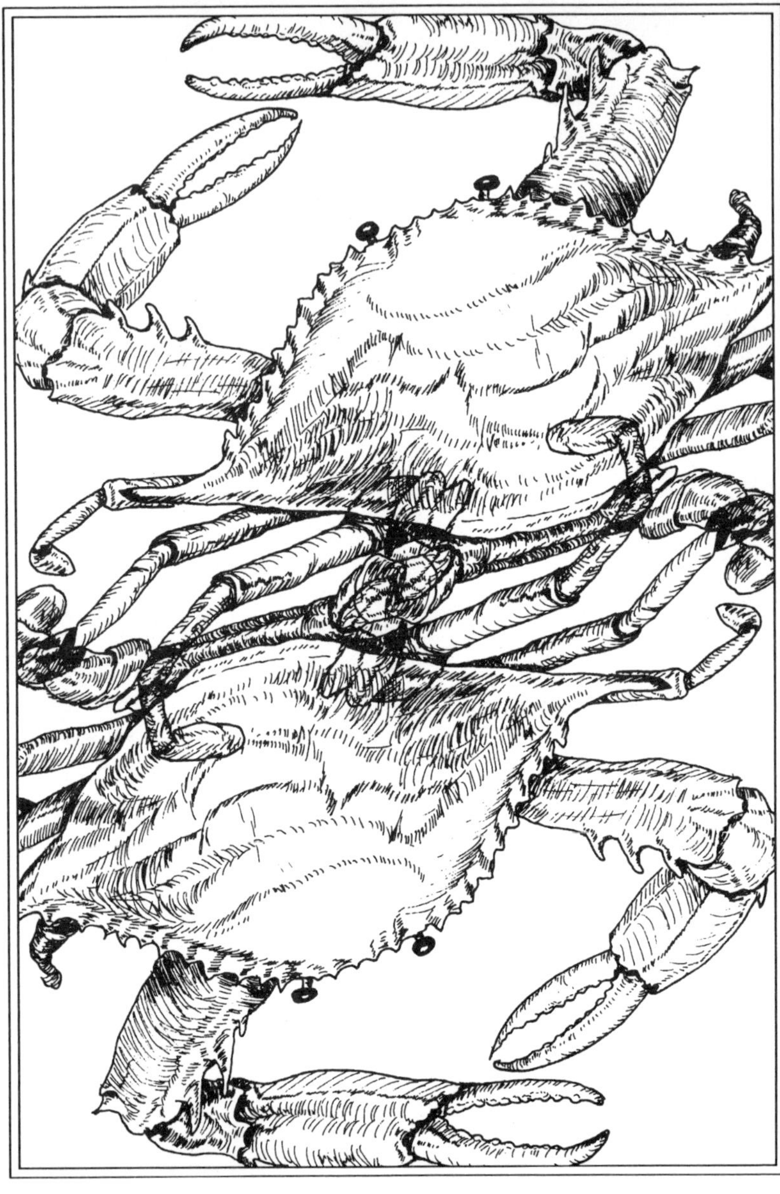